THE BIO____ ___

OF

DAVE MATTHEWS

The Rise of an American Musician from Humble
Beginnings to Global Stardom

Donald J. Martin

Copyright Donald J. Martin@2024All rights reserved. No part of this publication may be replicated, distributed, or transmitted in any manner, including photocopying, recording, or any electronic or mechanical means, without prior written authorization from the publisher, except for brief quotations included in critical reviews or specific noncommercial uses allowed by copyright law.

This book is a nonfiction work founded on the author's research and experiences. While every effort has been exerted to ensure the precision and comprehensiveness of the information provided, neither the author nor the publisher assumes responsibility for any errors, omissions, or damages resulting from the utilization of the information contained.

Table of contents

Introduction

The band's front man, Dave Matthews, has had an amazing life full of artistic expression, self-discovery, and intimate fan ties. Early years of Dave were greatly influenced by apartheid, a period of extreme division in South Africa. Raised in Johannesburg, South Africa, he has a wide musical background encompassing folk music, jazz, and African rhythms. For a comfort and escape from his difficult social surroundings, music grew very crucial in his life.

Moving to the United States when Dave was a tiny child was not a straightforward transition for his family. Though his new country posed new difficulties, he had fresh opportunities to explore his music more fully. When he finally made Charlottesville,

Virginia his home, he discovered circumstances fit for developing his artistic ability. Here, in the vibrant local music scene, he laid the groundwork for his future in music.

Dave Matthews wanted to start a band as his musical ability evolved. He started assembling a group of gifted musicians destined to form Dave Matthews Band. Members of the band helped to define their unique sound: Carter Beauford, Stefan Lessard, Boyd Tinsley, and LeRoi Moore Jazz, rock, folk, and world music taken together created a unique sound for the band. Following their debut presentations in Charlottesville, word of their unique, one-of-a-kind presentations traveled fast. Not soon after forming, the band received media attention and a sizable following.

Under the Table and Dreaming by Dave Matthews Band marked a game-changer. Popular tunes from the 1994 album, such as "Crash Into Me" and "What Would You Say," truly connected to listeners. The record's appeal helped the band to establish their position in the music industry. Their ensuing albums, Crash and Before These Crowded Streets, enhanced their status as a first-rate 90s band. The major CD hits stunned both reviewers and fans. Concurrently, the band gained recognition from their aggressive and emotionally charged live performances. Dave Matthews's engaging stage presence and ability to connect to his audience made every performance remarkable.

Celebrity came with difficulties, albeit as well. Being in the limelight came with some pressure as the band gained increasing popularity. Dave Matthews frequently questioned the challenge of remaining regular while surrounded with celebrities. Still, he kept himself in his music and in his thoughts, authoring songs that would appeal to listeners with all his whole attention.

Dave Matthews explored various interests outside of his band; he was never one to limit himself creatively. When his first solo album, Some Devil, released in 2003, he deviated from the band's vibrant approach. He received a Grammy for the slower, more private, quite personal song on the record, "Gravedigger." Having acted in films and TV, Dave Matthews also took part actively in the acting scene. His love of stories never wavered even as he explored using other media.Apart from his artistic endeavors, Matthews gained recognition for his charity. Among his various humanitarian endeavors is the Bama Works Fund he launched to further environmental and social justice. Both his songs and his deeds demonstrated his dedication to improve the earth as he often used his position to spread awareness of critical problems. Even if Matthews was well-known, he always placed his family first and maintained a great sense of balance in a life that might easily turn domineering.

Over the years, the Dave Matthews Band has grown rather popular. Their music has influenced millions of people all around; their concerts are still among the most iconic events in rock history. Many musicians today have mentioned Matthews as a source of inspiration, therefore proving his impact on contemporary rock music. Songs of the band have remained relevant over years, appealing to individuals from different walks of life. Their ability to stay faithful while also updating for the current era has kept their committed fanbase.

Dave Matthews wonders over the amazing trip he has gone over his career. Matthews has maintained a single focus on his music and the relationships he has developed with his fans during his meteoric climb from obscurity in South Africa to global recognition. Along with musicians, audiences of all ages will find inspiration in his legacy of passion, honesty, and inventiveness.

Chapter 1

Who is Dave Matthews?

Born during the trying apartheid era in Johannesburg, South Africa, Dave Matthews Growing up in a split society, he experienced the conflicts and difficulties of that age. Still, his family gave him great love and encouragement. South Africa's rich musical culture inspired Matthews from a broad spectrum of genres, including folk, jazz, and African rhythms. From early on, his enthusiasm for music was greatly shaped by this varied musical exposure.

Matthews's family moved to the United States when he was a teenager; this was an interesting and demanding change. Though it was difficult, adjusting to a new nation and culture gave him fresh chances to pursue his artistic passions. Matthews discovered a creative and encouraging environment in Charlottesville, Virginia, which would become very vital for his artistic growth. The music environment of the city provided him the ideal platform to follow his aspirations, and it was here Matthews started to confirm his road towards being the musician he is today.

The Early Life of Dave Matthews

Born in Johannesburg, South Africa, on January 9, 1967, Dave Matthews came of age during a period of severe apartheid control for the nation. Under apartheid, people of many races were treated quite differently since the regime legally enforced racial separation. Particularly Black South Africans were denied many fundamental rights and suffered extensive prejudice. This split impacted Dave's early years and grew him up in a milieu of tremendous conflict. Living in an apartheid country presented difficulties, but Dave's family set up an environment where he could flourish.

American fire safety engineer John Matthews was his father; his mother, Valerie, was from the United Kingdom. Having progressive opinions and strong opposition to apartheid, both parents pushed Dave to consider the society he lived in closely. Dave's parents developed his capacity to see beyond South Africa's racial divisions in a period when many others were swayed by the repressive apartheid government. Dave would always be guided by the moral principles they taught him—fairness, equality, and respect of all people. Growing up in this environment, Dave Matthews started to acquire a deep feeling of justice and compassion that would later shape his songs.

Although apartheid permeated all aspects of South African life, the nation nevertheless has a rich and varied culture, particularly in relation to music. Dave was early exposed to a range of musical genres, including African rhythms, jazz, folk, and rock. The music scene in Johannesburg was energetic and vivid; South Africa's songs combined traditions. Dave's taste of such a broad spectrum of sounds inspired his love of music and affected his eventual development of his own original style. The emotive and rhythmic elements of African music as well as the improvisational elements of jazz particularly drew him in. Growing up, the music he listened to would later motivate him in his work and help him to combine several genres into his unique sound.

Apart from the South African music he listened to, Dave also found influence in the tunes performed at his house. Deeply passionate about music, his father frequently turned on records by Miles Davis, Bob Dylan, and The Beatles. Dave was exposed to a great range of genres via these musical inspirations, and he came to value the richness and inventiveness of music from many throughout the globe. From his father, Dave also discovered the power of music as a means of expression and how it may unite people and function as a tool for narrative. Early exposure to both African music and Western performers shaped Dave's musical personality by combining several components into his own unique voice.

South Africa was a nation rife with conflict and inequality even if its musical legacy was rich. Dave Matthews started to notice the hardships his nation was experiencing as a small child. For millions of Black South Africans, who were governmentally methodically deprived, apartheid made daily existence challenging. Dave knew something was wrong with the way people treated others depending on their skin tone even as a small child. Dave developed his own ideas on justice and equality by means of frank conversations on the political environment in South Africa, which clearly showed opposition to apartheid by his family. He grew up in an environment that pushed him to examine the world around him and stand out for what is right even if he was too young to take part in demonstrations or campaigning.

Dave Matthews experienced a great personal loss at ten years old. 1977 saw the death from cancer of John Matthews, his father. Dave suffered much from this loss and had to grow fast. Having his father die at such a young age was a terrible event that helped Dave understand the value of love and family. As he investigated concepts of loss, longing, and personal introspection in his music, some of his later work would revolve on the grief he experienced. Dave Matthews displayed tenacity and strength in spite of the grief at losing his father; these qualities would serve him well in the years to come.

Dave's mother chose to relocate the family to the United States following the loss of his father. When the Matthews family moved to the United States in the early 1980s, Dave's life underwent a fresh turn. Dave was leaving behind everything he had known, hence his journey from South Africa to the United States was a significant one. Though it was difficult, learning to live in a foreign nation gave Dave new chances to pursue his passions and grow as a musician. Along with a sense of liberation from the racial divisions of apartheid, the relocation allowed Dave to live in another cultural environment.

Dave started more carefully investigating his musical abilities after the family moved to Charlottesville, Virginia. Small but energetic, Charlottesville gave Dave a creative space that would shape his future profession. He started to participate more in the local music scene here, and it was in Charlottesville that he started to build the basis for what would finally be the Dave Matthews Band. The music environment of the city mixed several genres, and Dave could relate to other artists driven by his love of music. Early years in Charlottesville were very important for determining his future as a musician since they gave him the time and encouragement he needed to develop as an artist.

Dave Matthews was impacted by various elements throughout his early years in South Africa, including the political environment, his family's ideals, and the varied music around him. His encounters in Johannesburg changed his perspective and enabled him to grow deeply sympathetic and fair. From African rhythms to jazz and rock, the music he heard growing up greatly shaped his destiny as a musician. His journey to the United States was a turning point in his life and would finally help him to rise to be among the most powerful musicians of his generation.

From early life, Dave Matthews was immersed in a rich and varied musical environment, which was rather crucial in developing his enthusiasm for music. Growing up in Johannesburg, South Africa, he came to a wide spectrum of musical styles that stayed with his sound and creative sense. Fundamental elements of South Africa's musical history were jazz, folk music, and African rhythms—all of which formed Matthews' musical sensibility.

Notwithstanding apartheid's hardships, South Africa's active musical landscape gave Matthews access to a mix of Western styles and traditional African music. For him, African music with its expressive melodies and intricate rhythms had a deep effect. Typical of South African music, the polyrhythmic beats and call-and-response patterns developed Matthews's respect for rhythm, a quality that would eventually define his own work. These components helped him come to see how music may express feelings and tell stories—something that would eventually define his songwriting.

Apart from indigenous African music, Matthews's jazz exposure broadened his musical horizons even more. Jazz spoke to him especially because of its emphasis on creative expression and improvisation. Through his father's record collection, he first heard jazz musicians such Miles Davis, John

Coltrane, and Thelonious Monk. The spontaneous quality of jazz let Matthews investigate fresh approaches of musical expression. Jazz's emphasis on individual originality and freedom to experiment motivated Matthews to take chances in his own music, combining several genres and sounds in a way only he could do.

Early musical growth of Matthews was greatly influenced by Western rock and folk music as well. His father was first exposed to rock and folk via his passion for musicians including The Beatles, Bob Dylan, and Neil Young. Matthews related to the emotional intensity of rock as well as the storytelling features of folk music. The Beatles especially had a great impact on him. Matthews was motivated to view music as a boundless means of expression by their creative approach to it and their ability to mix several genres and produce fresh sounds.

African rhythms, jazz improvisation, Western rock and folk—among other different musical inspirations—helped Matthews create a distinctive style. He learned to create something unique by combining elements of several musical traditions rather than limited to just one genre. Matthews's perspective of music as a potent weapon for expression was shaped in part by South Africa's rhythms, jazz's inventiveness, and the emotional depth of folk and rock. Later on, this basis would shape his work with the Dave Matthews Band, where he combined these several components to produce a unique sound appealing to millions of people worldwide.

These several musical inspirations also affected Matthews' technique to songwriting. Early on he discovered that music could be a tool for narrative, and he investigated social justice, love, and sorrow using his own compositions. Growing older, he started to build his own voice, drawing on these inspirations but producing something totally own. The rhythms and melodies he grew up with became part of his musical DNA.

Dave Matthews's early exposure to a range of musical genres was ultimately quite important in forming his love of music. His musical evolution was shaped by African music's rhythmic pulse, jazz's improvisational energy, and rock and folk's narrative elements. Matthews's varied musical experience enabled him to grow to have a strong awareness of music as an expressive, transforming power—an awareness that would direct him throughout his career and add to the Dave Matthews Band's distinctive sound.

Relocating to the United States

Early in the 1980s, Dave Matthews's life changed significantly when his family moved to the United States. At the time Matthews was 14 years old, hence leaving South Africa was not a simple choice. Following the personal loss of his father in 1977, the Matthews family decided to start over in another nation. This action was a significant change in Dave's life since it not only meant leaving behind the house he had known but also presented difficulties adjusting to a new culture, setting, and way of life. Matthews' development—personal as much as creative—was much enhanced by this change.

The challenges of life in South Africa during the apartheid era, where racial segregation and systematic discrimination were firmly ingrained, greatly shaped the Matthews family's choice to relocate. Although the relocation promised a fresh start, Matthews had to bid farewell to his boyhood house, friends, and only life he had known. Matthews had spent much of his early years in Johannesburg, a city permanently scarred by apartheid. Matthews's family was progressive in their ideas and believed in justice and equality, even if living in such a segregated culture presented difficulties. Matthews was profoundly affected by this viewpoint, which would accompany him all his life and shape his activism and song. Moving away from that setting into another universe, though, seemed intimidating.

In many respects, the United States stood a far cry from South Africa. Matthews was in a new cultural environment as a teen, one molded by different history, politics, and way of life. From a nation where racial tensions and divides were a daily occurrence to the

United States, the change brought radically different social dynamics. Though the United States had its own racial problems, it presented a new environment that let Matthews feel some degree of freedom not available in apartheid South Africa. That change was not without challenges, though.

Matthews' struggles stemmed mostly from the emotional toll of bidding farewell to everything known. Matthews had grown up in Johannesburg, and his personality was in great part shaped by the city and its inhabitants. Matthews was not just bereaved of his father but also of his friends and the cultural setting that had molded him when his family moved. Arriving in the United States at such a young age meant Matthews had to adjust to a different identity in a foreign environment. Managing this new reality while juggling the emotional weight of transition drove Matthews to grow up fast.

The family made their home in Charlottesville, Virginia, a major change from Johannesburg in many respects. Small and quieter than the busy metropolitan life Matthews had experienced, Charlottesville was a town. But it was also a place with a vibrant and encouraging artistic culture that would provide Matthews the creative license and inspiration he required. Moving to Charlottesville let him follow his passion in music with more concentration and autonomy since the town's music scene was active and gave local musicians a stage. For Matthews, this was a pivotal period when he started to give his musical aspirations significant attention. Though it was a small town, Charlottesville had a vibrant underground music culture, and Matthews soon got engaged with local artists, which would later help him create his own signature sound.

Initially, though, adjusting to life in Charlottesville was difficult. Matthews faced several difficulties from the cultural differences between South Africa and the United States, especially trying to blend in as an outsider into a new surroundings. From what Matthews had been used to in South Africa, the local customs, the speed of life, even the way people interacted with one another were different. His background as an immigrant added complexity to his navigating of the social dynamics of being a teen in a foreign nation. Matthews was acutely aware of how race affected social relationships as he had grown up in a segregated environment and had to redefine his conception of race and identity in order to fit the American terrain.

Matthews was also coping with the loss of his father, therefore adjusting not only to the customs of a foreign nation. Matthews had previously experienced loss from losing his father at a young age, and relocating to the United States without his father at hand made that loss much more noticeable. The change made Matthews more introspective and self-dependent, and his songs captured the emotional upheavals of this age. This period of emotional crisis shaped many of the subjects of his songs, including grief, longing, and seeking personal significance.

Still, the difficulties Matthews encountered during this period of adaptation also helped him develop personally. The process of learning to live in the United States helped him to grow more self-aware. Matthews started to view his own experiences differently even if he was surrounded with cultural isolation. Through his songs, he started to explore his loss, displacement, and identity and become more aware of the world around him. Later on, his growing awareness of his emotions would enable him to create songs having broad relevance in addition to being rather intimate.

Although challenging, Matthews' progress as an artist was much enhanced by his move to the United States. Matthews discovered a creative release in Charlottesville that helped him explore his musical abilities in a way never possible in Johannesburg. The U.S.'s cultural openness led Matthews to work with a varied collection of musicians and freely explore several genres. Matthews started developing the musical identity that would define the Dave Matthews Band here by combining elements from his new American environment and South African background.

In Matthews' life, this time of change represented a pivotal turning point. He started to find his identity as a musician and personally throughout this period of adaptation and emotional development. Along with the loss of his father, the difficulties of moving to the United States drove Matthews to grow in ways that would eventually impact his music. His career as one of the most distinctive and powerful musicians of his generation would start with the emotional depth he developed during this period and his exposure to fresh musical influences.

His Formative Years in Charlottesville

Dave Matthews and his family moved from South Africa to the United States in the early 1980s, then settled in Charlottesville, Virginia. Matthews's creative development and the basis of his musical career were greatly influenced by this small town, which offered a special fusion of Southern appeal and active arts environment. Though Charlottesville was somewhat different from Johannesburg, the place gave Matthews the chances and surroundings he required to start defining his musical individuality.

Matthews found Charlottesville's close-knit community and rich history to provide a different pace of life than the busy city of Johannesburg. Although the journey from

South Africa to the United States was challenging in many respects, Charlottesville gave an environment that enabled him to concentrate on his artistic development. Matthews started to lose himself in the local music culture, far more approachable than the music business he had experienced in South Africa. For a young artist like Matthews to experiment, meet other artists, and start laying the groundwork for his career as a performer and songwriter, the town's music scene was ideal.

A major component of Charlottesville's impact on Matthews was the town's vibrant local music culture. Charlottesville, for all its tiny scale, had a vibrant musical culture that fit Matthews, who was only starting to discover his artistic voice. Local bands and artists could perform and highlight their skills at the several music venues in the town. Matthews joined this environment right away, performing in neighborhood bands and networking with other musicians that also loved music. Early partnerships allowed Matthews to refine his musical abilities and laid the groundwork for what would eventually be the Dave Matthews Band.

Matthews' music was much shaped by the creative freedom he encountered in Charlottesville. Smaller, more personal music venues in the community let him explore several sounds, styles, and songwriting approaches. For Matthews, this period of artistic inquiry was vital since it allowed him the time to discover his own voice. In many respects, Charlottesville became a venue where Matthews could explore his musical inspirations by fusing jazz, rock, folk, African rhythms into something fresh and personal. With the Dave Matthews Band, this mixing of genres would become a trademark of his upcoming output.

Charlottesville also was known for being a center of intellectual and cultural activity. Nestled in the center of the town, the University of Virginia attracted a varied student and artist population that enhanced the creative energy of the community. Another significant impact on Matthews was Charlottesville's ethnic variety. Both musically and socially, he was exposed to a range of points of view that helped him to widen his horizons. The intellectual and creative surroundings of the town inspired Matthews, and this exposure to many ideas and points of view helped his songwriting to be more deep and complicated.

Matthews' development during his early years in Charlottesville was also greatly influenced by the community the town provided. Local musicians, venues, and music fans' support enabled Matthews to develop as a performer. Early years in the United States were mostly shaped by this feeling of belonging to a small but fervent music community. It gave him the assurance to keep following music despite the difficulties of beginning anew in a foreign nation. Matthews's experiences in Charlottesville not only developed his musical skills but also strengthened his conviction in the value of community and teamwork, which would eventually become major subjects in his work.

Matthews developed professional contacts and friendships in Charlottesville that also prepared the way the Dave Matthews Band came to be. Matthews first met several of the players who would eventually form the band in this town, including bassist Stefan Lessard and drummer Carter Beauford. Matthews was able to collaborate with other gifted musicians in Charlottesville, and it was during this period that he started developing the concepts that would finally result in the founding of the band. The local music environment of the area provided Matthews the chance to discover his voice as a songwriter and performer as well as the confidence he needed to go professional in music.

For Matthews, Charlottesville also gave him consistency amid a period of tremendous personal transformation. Matthews was still getting used to life in the United States after leaving South Africa as a teen. The little village gave a slower pace of life that let him concentrate on his music and also give a feeling of grounding. Matthews first settled in Charlottesville during his early years in the United States; it was here he started to lay the groundwork for the music career that would eventually bring him worldwide recognition.

Matthews became rather attached to Charlottesville and its people over his stay. His encounters in this town changed his perspective in addition to his artistic approach. Matthews discovered the resources and inspiration he required to pursue a career in music in Charlottesville from the artistic surroundings, local music culture, and feeling of community. Matthews started to take music seriously in Charlottesville, where he also established the foundation for the Dave Matthews Band to grow and eventually alter the path of rock music.

For Matthews, Charlottesville was in many respects a creative incubator. It was where his musical ideas initially started to develop and where he could interact with other musicians that aligned with his vision. Matthews had the freedom in the friendly town to develop and experiment as an artist. Matthews's music and his personality as an artist were greatly shaped by his formative years in Charlottesville, which also prepared the ground for the success to follow in the next years.

Chapter 2

His Moment in Birth of the Dave Matthews Band

The Dave Matthews Band marks a turning point in the development of contemporary rock music. Early in the 1990s, Matthews started his vision to establish a distinctive musical collective out of his increasing need to establish a band able to combine several musical inspirations. Matthews aimed to gather a group of gifted musicians that shared his love of producing unique sounds after years of experimenting and gigs in Charlottesville local bands.

The Dave Matthews Band's identity was much shaped by the four core members: Carter Beauford, Stefan Lessard, Boyd Tinsley, and LeRoi Moore. Key to the group's unique approach were Beauford's drums, Lessard's basslines, Tinsley's violin, and Moore's saxophone. Their musical chemistry set the groundwork for what would turn out to be a revolutionary fusion of global music, folk, jazz, and rock.

Though their early gigs in Charlottesville were small, word-of-mouth soon spread and local listeners were drawn to the band's distinctive sound. Their fan base expanded as they kept performing at nearby places, opening the path for their breakthrough in the music business and ultimately helping them to become rather famous.

How His vision in forming the Band Takes Shape

Dave Matthews, a solo artist who had already been penning and performing songs, began to sense a mounting need to go in another direction in the early 1990s. Years of honing his solo performance abilities had gone toward him, but now he yearned to work with other musicians to produce something more powerful and grand. Matthews saw a band able to create a unique sound by combining a great range of musical influences—from rock and jazz to folk and world music. He knew that his musical path would take him working with talented musicians who shared his love of invention and determination to challenge limits.

Matthews was already residing in Charlottesville, Virginia, a town with a strong and active local music culture despite its modest population. Matthews found the little musical scene in Charlottesville to be the perfect setting for him to begin assembling his band. He started visiting neighborhood places and meeting gifted musicians that also loved experimenting and music. Matthews understood that the special sound he was thinking of would call for much more than just his guitar and vocals. He wanted musicians who could offer fresh layers to his compositions and match his style, those who could bring their own thoughts and abilities to the music.

Matthews first worked with exceptionally talented drummer Carter Beauford, whose extraordinary technique and adaptability are well-known. Beauford fit Matthews' changing musical vision since she had already performed in several bands. Beauford's jazz-based drumming technique appealed to Matthews since it could readily fit rock and other genres, but it was originally Beauford stood out because of his ability to play with both accuracy and passion; Matthews knew that the sound of the band would depend much on his drumming. The two players started performing together and soon found great musical compatibility. Matthews recognized that Beauford's contributions would propel the music forward, and it was not long before he realized Beauford would be a major player in the upcoming band.

Matthews started looking for other musicians to cover the remaining band parts shortly after meeting Beauford. Matthews was first drawn to teenage bassist Stefan Lessard because of his talent and sense of rhythm. Lessard was naturally able to produce rich, funky basslines that fit Beauford's drumming exactly. Lessard's approach accentuated Matthews' acoustic guitar performance, giving the song foundation and richness. Matthews thought Lessard was a great fit for his goal of combining several musical genres since he appreciated her ability to adjust to many musical genres while keeping a strong feeling of rhythm.

Matthews went to Boyd Tinsley, a violinist whose special tone would be greatly shaped by Beauford and Lessard on board. The way Tinsley handled the violin was unlike anything Matthews had ever seen. The unique sound of the band was created in great part by Tinsley's improvisation and violin blending with rock and jazz music. Matthews valued Tinsley's audacity to challenge the limits of what a violin could accomplish in a rock band environment.

Tinsley's performance gave the song an ethereal and soulful character, therefore adding a depth of complexity unique to the band among others in the music scene.

At last, Matthews went for LeRoi Moore, a saxophonist steeped in jazz and classical music. Moore's saxophone playing gave the band's sound a lyrical, fluid quality. His ability to create spontaneous solos and complex melodies gave the band's sound still another level of richness. Matthews said Moore's performance complemented the rest of the band's lineup perfectly since it gave the typically high-energy, improvisational concerts some soul and heart. The band's distinctive texture derived from Moore's musical background helped them to stand out from other rock bands of the day.

The picture for the band started to take shape as Matthews started to put together this gifted collection of players. Matthews's basic concept was to establish a musical collective whereby every member could add their own originality and impact while cooperating to produce a sound that was fresh, inventive, and really collaborative. Matthews was ready to combine his folk-rock background with the several genres that shaped him—jazz, classical, world music, and so on. He considered the band as a place for experimentation where every member's opinion was appreciated and where the music could be always changing.

Forming the band had certain difficulties as well. Matthews had a particular sound in mind, but the band struggled to get going. Early sessions were full of trial and error as the group worked to combine their unique approaches. Matthews had to believe that the long hours spent practicing and experimenting would eventually pay off and that the chemistry among the musicians would produce something unique. The band members started to create a distinctive sound combining aspects of rock, jazz, folk, and world music as they started to perform together more often.

The band members' success depended critically on their cooperation. Matthews saw the band as a whole, not as a project driven by his own vision; he was receptive to the Ideas and efforts of every player. This cooperative attitude helped the band develop camaraderie and the members started to create strong creative relationships that would define the band's direction. Matthews saw that the secret to success would not only be in producing outstanding music but also in designing a setting where every member may flourish and add to the general tone of the band.

Matthews discovered he had found a group of musicians who matched his love of stretching musical limits as his idea for the band started to take shape. Matthews had put together a band with Carter Beauford on drums, Stefan Lessard on bass, Boyd Tinsley on violin, and LeRoi Moore on saxophone that was not just gifted but also eager to experiment and take chances. Together, they started to produce a sound that was absolutely distinctive—one that would eventually come to define the Dave Matthews Band's characteristic approach.

Their songs combined several genres, fusing rock with jazz, folk with global rhythms, and improvisation with methodically written songs. This mix of influences would define the band's unique sound, and it was abundantly evident that Matthews's choice to start a band had produced something unique—a group capable of producing complex yet approachable, spontaneous yet disciplined music. Matthews had been successful in gathering musicians who aligned with his vision, and taken together, they would alter the landscape of contemporary rock music.

How He selected the Core Members

Realizing his vision required Dave Matthews to choose the appropriate musicians when he started building the ensemble that would finally be the Dave Matthews ensemble. Matthews understood that his sound would only be effective if he surrounded himself with really talented, adaptable musicians who could contribute their special skills. He sought musicians that could complement his own playing style, explore several genres, and produce something original and creative, not only ones who could perform well. Matthews carefully chose every one of the essential players—Carter Beauford, Stefan Lessard, Boyd Tinsley, and LeRoi Moore—in his quest for the ideal lineup.

Among the first artists Matthews decided to collaborate with was percussionist Carter

Beauford. Beauford was well-known in the neighborhood Charlottesville music scene for his flawless technique and broad genre-spanning performance prowess. Beauford's distinctive drumming technique—which combined jazz, funk, and rock—along with his accuracy and expressive playing captivated Matthews. Beauford was a master of crafting complicated but understandable rhythms that precisely matched Matthews's goal to produce music with great complexity and energy. The instant synergy between Matthews and Beauford made it very evident that Beauford's drumming would define the sound of the band. The band's varied musical approach was shaped in part by his inventiveness and flexibility in adjusting to several musical genres.

Stefan Lessard, a young bassist whose capacity to lock in with Beauford's complex rhythms anchored the band's sound, was the second essential member Matthews chose. Having seen Lessard perform in neighborhood Charlottesville bands, Matthews was particularly struck with his musical maturity—especially for someone so young. Lessard naturally could combine the sophisticated rhythms and melodies Matthews was aiming for with deep, funky basslines. Matthews valued Lessard's sense of time and his ability to give the music subdued but necessary layers. Lessard picked up Matthews' musical ideas and adjusted to the band's often changing sound, thus he was also fast learning. Lessard, the bassist, provided the harmonic and rhythmic depth needed to let the other members shine, hence strengthening the band's basis.

The band also needed the violinist Boyd Tinsley. Matthews envisioned combining rock and jazz with classical and folk components, and Tinsley's violin work uniquely brought those genres together. Matthews particularly appreciated Tinsley's adaptability and skill in including improvisation into his performance. Unlike other rock bands of the era, the band's music felt spacious and textured because of the ethereal and melodic qualities of the violin. Tinsley took chances, playing in a creative and expressive manner, not limited by conventional classical performance. His classical background and improvisational style let the band's sound to grow more wide, straying between soft, melodic lines and forceful, energizing solos. Matthews considered Tinsley as the ideal fit for his vision of a band able to combine several genres, and his contribution became a distinctive quality of the band's sound.

LeRoi Moore, a saxophone whose jazz music knowledge gave the band's musical approach still another level of sophistication and depth, was the last member Matthews selected. Moore's rich, soulful saxophone added the band's music a smooth, melodic character. Matthews considered technical ability and emotional depth to be absolutely vital for the band's sound, hence he was able to perform both of them. Moore had a background in jazz, and the band's live shows—where improvisation was central—depended on his easy ability to improvise. Matthews respected Moore's musicianship and his capacity to fit the often shifting character of their performances. Whether Moore was playing more forceful, experimental solos or beautiful, soothing melodies, his saxophone lines melted naturally with the other instruments. His performance gave the band's sound a special texture, therefore raising the degree of intricacy in their songs.

These fundamental members combined their unique skills and abilities for the band, hence forming the unique sound of the Dave Matthews Band. Matthews's choice to choose musicians with not just great technical ability but also great creative ability helped the band produce a really original sound. Beauford's complex rhythms, Lessard's strong bass foundation, Tinsley's expressive violin, and Moore's soulful saxophone combined to provide a dynamic, multi-layered musical experience. Matthews wanted the band to be a place where every member could provide ideas, challenge genre norms, and try new sounds. Matthews had gathered a team capable of realizing his goal with these four fundamental components.

Every band member was instrumental in blending rock, jazz, folk, and world music to establish the sound of the band. Lessard's bass anchored the music with its deep grooves, Beauford's drumming added complexity and energy, Tinsley's violin offered both texture and melody, and Moore's saxophone gave the mix a soulful, jazzy quality. It was evident as Matthews assembled these musicians that this group was meant to be unique. The Dave Matthews Band's popularity began with the synergy between Matthews and his core members; their musical partnership would go on to define the band's sound for years to come.

His Vision in Building a Unique Sound

Dave Matthews aspired to create a distinctive sound using a broad range of musical inspirations, not only another rock band when he started out forming the Dave Matthews Band. Matthews thought that music should be about experimenting and combining several genres in novel ways never done before. His aim was to produce something fresh, interesting, and really unique so the band's sound would be memorable in a packed music scene. Jazz, rock, folk, and world music Matthews brought to the table would be quite important in determining the band's character and the sound that would finally become famous.

Among the genres most significantly influencing the band's sound was jazz. The improvisational and free-flowing character of jazz music had long captivated Matthews. Jazz performers' capacity to express themselves in the moment, taking chances and producing dynamic, erratic music appealed to him. The Dave Matthews Band's live performances, where the members frequently engaged in long, unplanned jams, became increasingly dependent on this improvisational energy. Matthews urged the group to break away from the limitations of conventional song forms by experimenting with new creative approaches and bold ideas. Jazz is clearly audible in the band's sophisticated rhythms, sophisticated time signatures, and the way the members sometimes played off one another on live events. With his ability to include intricate rhythms and syncopations into the music, Drummer Carter Beauford—who had a great foundation in jazz—was very helpful in giving the band this flavor.

Drawing on the passion and force of rock music, Matthews also desired the band's sound to have strong rock roots at the same time. Although the band experimented with other genres, Matthews and his friends understood they wanted to produce songs with catchy melodies and bold, expressive lyrics that would appeal to rock listeners. With electric guitar riffs, powerful bass lines, and vigorous percussion, this rock influence provided the band's music a strong basis. Lead singer and guitarist Matthews blended his passion for rock music with his own songwriting technique. Often marked by repetitive strumming and percussion, his guitar playing produced a sound grounded yet energetic. Jazz and rock elements combined to provide the band a flexibility that let them alternate between passionate, high-energy passages and more subdued, reflective parts inside one song.

Folk music has still another significant impact on the band's sound. Matthews himself had grown up listening to folk musicians whose musical simplicity and narrative really connected with him. Joni Mitchell and Bob Dylan were among them. Matthews's songwriting style, which frequently centers on personal experiences, social themes, and emotional storytelling, was shaped by the importance placed by folk music on lyrics, acoustic instruments, and simple yet strong melodies. Along with the quieter, more introspective passages in their songs, the band's sound reflects Matthews's folk inspirations by including acoustic guitar. A trademark of the Dave Matthews Band's music is their ability to combine acoustic and electronic components to produce a sound anchored in traditional folk structures and overlaid with sophisticated equipment. Matthews frequently wrote with an eye toward vivid imagery, emotions, and profound personal introspection, so the lyrical content of the band's songs is shaped by folk's narrative impact.

Apart from jazz, rock, and folk, Matthews was greatly inspired by world music, which grew to be another essential element forming the distinctive sound of the band. World music, which spans many worldwide musical traditions, let the band explore rhythms, melodies, and instrumentation from many civilizations. Through rhythmic patterns, percussion instruments, and melodic structures, Matthews and his colleagues were particularly drawn to African, Latin, and Caribbean inspirations they included into their music. The band's usage of syncopated beats and sophisticated polyrhythms—often inspired by African and Latin rhythms—showcases this impact. By including world music, the band gave its songs a distinctive taste and produced a sound that seemed worldwide and vast. World music's rhythmic thrust also fit Matthews's idea of producing a dynamic and always changing musical experience in which the rhythm section was important in advancing the song forward.

Jazz, rock, folk, and world music were not always easy additions for the band's sound, and developing their trademark style took time. Matthews worked with several combinations of these inspirations in the early days in search of the ideal harmony among them. Developing the unique sound of the band was mostly dependent on their eagerness to explore and take chances. Matthews let his members contribute their own musical inspirations, therefore enabling the band's sound to change naturally. The band gained recognition over time for their ability to seamlessly combine genres in a way that felt natural, therefore producing a sound all their own.

The Dave Matthews Band's sound is particularly distinguished by their use of improvisation. Matthews and his friends thought that every performance presented an opportunity to produce fresh ideas, hence they frequently performed their songs in several ways every time. Every night the band's songs gained fresh life thanks to their improvised style allowing them to explore several musical spheres. Jazz improvisation combined with rock intensity, folk storytelling, and global rhythms created a fresh and erratic sound that would excite and spontaneity every performance would have. One of the defining features of the

Dave Matthews Band's music became their capacity to combine genres and let improvisation flourish.

Dave Matthews envisioned the band continuously pushing the envelope of genre and producing something fresh and original. Jazz, rock, folk, and world music combined to let the band create a sophisticated but approachable, vibrant but thoughtful sound. Matthews's passion of experimenting and teamwork with his gifted bandmates produced a sound that would define the band's future and impact next generations of artists. Combining these several musical components produced a sound unlike anything else in the music scene, which came to define the Dave Matthews Band.

How Led the First Performances in the Road to Recognition

Particularly in their hometown of Charlottesville, Virginia, the Dave Matthews Band's early performances were absolutely vital in their ascent to popularity. These first performances prepared the ground for their ultimate national and international success as well as for what would become a legendary career. Early band performances were distinguished by a mix of raw intensity, musical inventiveness, and audience connection—qualities that would define their career going forward.

Dave Matthews was already building a reputation in Charlottesville as a talented musician before he launched the band. Matthews first became well-known for his solo, intimate, personal shows stressing his guitar and creative skills. Matthews started performing with a group of local musicians like Carter Beauford, Stefan Lessard, Boyd Tinsley, and LeRoi Moore, all of whom brought their unique musical qualities to the mix after he decided to create a full band. The band's diverse inspirations and open attitude to experimenting helped them to become well-known in the local music scene quite quickly.

The band's earliest gigs were somewhat modest, usually in little venues like neighborhood taverns and clubs in Charlottesville. Early performances were characterized by spontaneity; the band frequently experimented with fresh ideas and improvised. The band was still working on their sound, hence every concert allowed them to improve their chemistry and establish rapport with their audience. These shows proved not only their musical prowess but also their capacity for interacting with their audience. On stage, Matthews had a natural charm that would later define their live performances and assist to establish an emotional link between the band and the audience.

As the band performed more often in the neighborhood scene, word-of-mouth started to circulate. Different from other local bands, their distinctive sound combined rock, jazz, folk, and world music elements. Show attendees were fast to communicate their enthusiasm with others, and before long the band's appeal started to rise. The band gained a devoted following in Charlottesville right away for their ability to produce a live performance experience with both musically sophisticated complexity and emotional appeal. Along with the music, people started flocking to their performances for the excitement and energy the band injected into the stage.

Growing popularity of Matthews and the band was mostly due to their emphasis on improvisation. The Dave Matthews Band was well-known for deviating from many other bands that performed their songs exactly every night. Often changing with new solos, long jams, and unique takes on well-known songs, the songs would grow. The band's live performances seemed like an event, something that fans would enthusiastically await and would discuss long after the performance because of its spontaneity and unpredictability. In a crowded music scene, where many bands were performing simpler, predictable sets, it also allowed the band to stand out.

People outside of Charlottesville started to notice the band as their local appeal developed. Attracting music industry professionals and fans from surrounding cities, their performances at local venues such the Trax nightclub rapidly established them as one of the most interesting new bands in the region. The buzz of word-of-mouth about the band's live events started to expand, and soon they were performing in greater venues to front bigger audiences. As the band developed their abilities and grew their audience, their shows in Charlottesville and the surrounding area grew increasingly regular.

The band had one of their breakthrough moments when they recorded their first demo to help them advertise somewhere outside of Charlottesville. Matthews and the band understood it was time to move forward given their rising appeal in the local music industry. They started to concentrate on distributing their music to a larger audience, and their capacity to do so was much enhanced by the demo. Major record companies and music promoters were drawn to the tape, and soon the band was under demand from business people seeing their potential. The demo finally resulted in the band's first big deal, signed with RCA Records in 1993, therefore confirming their presence in the national music scene.

The band's early ascent to popularity also saw another turning point when they were invited to play the esteemed 1993 "Lollapalooza" event. For the band, this was a great chance since it let them play in front of a far bigger national audience. Being on the schedule was obvious evidence that the Dave Matthews Band had arrived since at the time Lollapalooza was among the most important music events in the United States. Their performance at Lollapalooza exposed audiences who had never seen them perform before and helped to confirm their image as a rising artist. The band stood out on the tour and their attractiveness was enhanced by their capacity to perform with vigor and improvisation at a big event.

Early events in Charlottesville, word-of-mouth reputation, and breakthrough events like the demo and Lollapalooza helped the Dave Matthews Band become nationally known. The band had developed a devoted following and a reputation for live performance by the time their first album, "Under the Table and Dreaming", came out in 1994. Their increasing popularity attested to their capacity to relate to their audience, their commitment to musical experimentation, and their unrelenting work ethic. Matthews and the band distinguished themselves from many other bands in these early years by stressing live performance, improvisation, and producing a distinctive musical

72

experience. Their shows' vitality combined with their creative approach to music allowed them to build a devoted audience that would keep expanding as they acquired national and worldwide respect. These early gigs started what would turn out to be one of the most successful and powerful careers in contemporary rock music.

Chapter 3

His Rise to Stardom

Early in the 1990s, Dave Matthews established the Dave Matthews Band (DMB) in Charlottesville, Virginia, so starting his ascent to popularity. His career underwent a sea change with his 1994 first album, "Under the Table and Dreaming". Unique recording for the album combined jazz, rock, and folk inspirations. The songs covered social and personal concerns including love, identity, and self-discovery. Success on the charts and with critics helped DMB become among the most creative and unique bands of the day.

Albums like "Crash" (1996) and "Before These Crowded Streets" (1998) thereafter confirmed DMB's position in rock history. With singles like "Crash Into Me" and "The

Space Between," which became anthems, these albums kept highlighting Matthews' compositional depth and received critical praise. The outstanding live performances of the band enhanced their success.

The live performances of DMB are renowned for their intensity and improvisational approach, which fosters close relationships with their audience. Though he struggles with sudden celebrity, Matthews has thought about the demands of popularity and emphasizes keeping personal balance while honoring his musical background.

His Debut Album through *Under the Table and Dreaming*

With the publishing of their first album, Under the Table and Dreaming, on 27th of September, 1994, he and the Dave Matthews Band (DMB) set off an incredible journey. Thanks to their vibrant live performances, the band had become relatively well-known in Charlottesville, Virginia, during the recording session. Originally from South Africa, Matthews brought a varied range of inspirations—jazz, folk, and rock among other things—which shaped the band's style. Steve Lillywhite, well-known for his work with U2, oversaw the album's production and his direction helped the band to develop their own approach. The recording sessions were a period of inquiry and discovery, and the outcome was an album that combined genres in a way never seen in the grunge and alternative rock dominated mid-90s music scene.

Under the Table and Dreaming's varied sound— Matthews combined rock, jazz, funk, and worldbeat components in unexpected and inventive ways—stood out. Using a range of instruments—everything from acoustic guitars to violin, saxophone, and percussion—that enhanced its rich, textured sound, the album's production was lush and deep. Matthews's emotive and occasionally mysterious songs, which spanned from introspection on love and personal development to more thorough social commentary, accentuated this originality. The album was more about a musical journey inviting listeners to interact with every track in their own way than it was about a single genre or style. This CD distinguished itself from other songs of the time since it defied easy box fit.

Lyrically, the tracks on Under the Table and Dreaming combined societal consciousness with love and introspection. Drawing on his own thoughts and experiences, Matthews' songs were frequently reflective and beautiful. Among the album's best songs, "Crash Into Me," became the band's defining song and is now among their most cherished singles. Audiences responded strongly to the song, which became an anthem of sorts for band fans with its seductive lyrics about love and longing. Many times, it is considered as a meditation on emotional closeness and the vulnerability inherent in a marriage. Another important song, "What Would You Say," addressed personal integrity and honesty, pushing listeners to examine their own motives and behavior. One of the most unforgettable songs on the record, the groovy rhythms and appealing chorus gave the message more intensity.

"Satellite" was still another song that highlighted Matthews' ability to use his words to produce emotional depth. The band's complex musical arrangement, which combined soft acoustic guitar with strong percussion and brass, highlighted the song's longing and search for something more than oneself theme. DMB's music was distinguished from other bands of the period by the combination of lively rhythms and intelligent lyrics. In the same vein, "The Best of What is Around" celebrated the present moment and exhorted listeners to value the beauty of life—even in the midst of uncertainty—so augmenting the more hopeful tone of the album.

Under the Table and Dreaming acquired popularity over time despite its first financial difficulties due to DMB's explosive live presentations. Before the album's release, the band's reputation as a live act had already started to travel; their devoted following helped drive the record higher on the charts. Its success came from the band's natural rise in popularity via word-of-mouth and their reputation for producing strong, unforgettable live performances, not from heavy radio play or promotional push. The record thus went on to reach multi-platinum level, confirming the band's position in the music scene.

Under the Table and Dreaming had broad effects. At a period when grunge and alternative rock ruled the music industry, DMB's original mix of genres and sophisticated musicianship gave popular music a fresh sound. The popularity of the album also signaled the start of the band's continuous interaction with their fans, based on live events and a shared community. Though universal, the band's personal approach let listeners relate to the songs and band on a closer level. Matthews's ability to combine personal introspection with more general society topics helped DMB appeal to a wider spectrum of listeners, and the album's variety guaranteed that it connected with people from many musical backgrounds.

Since DMB's music was frequently based on live improvisation and their shows were recognized for changing over time, the record also had a significant influence on the "jam band" movement's evolution. Under the Table and Dreaming's popularity spawned a new wave of jam bands embracing long, experimental live sets and mixed musical influences. Matthews's dedication to improvisation and spontaneity became DMB's trademark, and in the years to come this emphasis on the live experience will define the band.

Under the Table and Dreaming was ultimately a declaration of artistic vision and a mirror of the band's original approach to music, not only a debut album. Its impact went well beyond the early triumph it discovered in the 90s. Combining several genres and providing a new venue for artists who defied the mainstream, the record helped define the sound of alternative rock. Under the Table and Dreaming a historic release was made possible by Matthews's creative lyrics, inventive musical arrangements, and passionate live performances of the band. These elements also helped to establish the path for the band's ongoing success in the next few years.

His Chart-Topping Success

With highly praised and financially successful albums such "Crash" (1996) and "Before These Crowded Streets" (1998), lead singer and main songwriter Dave Matthews (DMB) attained celebrity status. The commercial success of the record was significantly influenced by a combination of straightforward melodies and sophisticated musical arrangements. Still among the band's best-selling albums in the US, the one becomes multi-platinum there.

The best song the band wrote, "Crash Into Me," gained notoriety for its emotional and passionate quality. This song became among DMB's most well-known singles and acquired great popularity with its eerie guitar riff, expressive words, and creepy melodies. Songs like "Too Much" and "So Much to Say" drove the band's even more general appeal. These songs' mix of rock and folk components helped them to become well-known and highlighted Matthews's ability to create catchy melodies with complex and convoluted emotional content.

Critics' initial response was one of wonder at "Crash"'s deft mix of genres. Matthews and his friends deftly combined jazz, rock, and global music with traditional folk themes. Steve Lillywhite, the album producer, got great accolades for both honing the band's sound for radio play and capturing their explosive live performances. Despite early misgivings from critics about the band's radio-friendly appeal, DMB showed with "Crash" that they could both push themselves creatively and profitably. The success of the album reflected a larger cultural phenomena as alternative rock evolved to include a greater spectrum of musical influences in the 1990s. Leading proponent of this movement was DMB. Live, the band was renowned for its improvisational energy and deep music; listeners connected with Matthews' meditative and even mysterious lyrics.

Released on April 28, 1998, the band's follow-up album, "Before These Crowded Streets", showed a more creative and daring side. Penetration of the "Billboard" 200 at No. 1 showed DMB's rejection to rely just on their commercial success. Rather, they sought to explore novel sounds, stretching the possibilities of rock music at the moment. Major inspirations were jazz, folk, and world music; the record distinguished itself with more intricate song structures and tighter musical arrangements. Building on the sound set by "Crash",

Matthews and his friends experimented with lengthier tracks and more complicated arrangements on "Before These Crowded Streets". Eastern and African rhythms were among the several musical traditions from which the record included unusual time signatures and sophisticated orchestration. Under closer inspection, these components produced a more difficult and gratifying listening experience with deep layers than its predecessor.

"Do not Drink the Water," the album's first success, most aptly captured the band's melancholy, introspective attitude. Apart from the more simple rock sound of "Crash"Matthews's narrative lyrics, the band's complex musicianship, and strong, depressing mood set apart this work. With lyrical images that suggested emotional weight and intensity, Matthews went into themes of human suffering and dislocation in this song. "Stay (Wasting Time)," another amazing song, had electric and acoustic components as well as longer instrumental passages that let the band's talent show. The long outro, which demonstrated the band's improvisational quality and the entertainment value of their live performances, was well enjoyed by the fans.

Though it lacked as many smash singles on the radio, most people felt "Before These Crowded Streets" was a better, more mature album than "Crash". Reviewers commended the album's breadth and asserted it revealed a more sophisticated side of the band, one free in its search of fresh ideas and sounds. Once more, Steve Lillywhite's production team deserves compliments for the album's meticulousness and richness of the songs. The album's distinctive sound resulted from the band recording it at several sites as well. Although the more experimental approach of the album may have turned off casual listeners, it was just this feature that attracted praise from critics and became a fan favorite.

Songs like "Pig" and "The Stone" highlighted the band's developing musical sophistication and Matthews' ability to translate very personal stories into ageless ideas. Because of its long instrumental sections and nonstandard time signature use, some have likened the album's musicality to jazz. Critics recognized this complexity as evidence of the band's development as musicians since it set out from the simpler rock of "Crash". More than just an album, "Before These Crowded Streets" mirrored the band's will to keep expanding and innovating new aural territory.

Thanks in large part to "Crash" and "Before These Crowded Streets"Dave Matthews Band gained popularity in the '90s and '00s. Although "Before These Crowded Streets" showed the band's adaptability outside of radio singles, "Crash" first brought them to the attention of mass listeners. These albums highlighted the band's extraordinary musicianship, Matthews's compositional mastery, and his ability to meld genres. Both albums received very positive response; "Crash"'s "Therefore Much to Say" won Best Rock Performance by a Duo or Group with Vocal, therefore earning the singer a Grammy. Though it lacked the same degree of economic success, "Before These Crowded Streets" was hailed as a more mature and ambitious record that stretched the band's creative horizons.

Dave Matthews Band defined the late '90s and early '00s rock scene with the aid of these records. Combining intricate musically with emotionally expressive lyrics let them appeal to a big audience while preserving a degree of creative integrity unique among many of their contemporaries. Both "Crash" and "Before These Crowded Streets" were critically successful, therefore confirming DMB's famous rock band reputation and proving their ongoing influence on the music industry.

How He Led Live Performances

Long praised for their explosive live performances, Dave Matthews Band (DMB) has been fundamental in the band's success and character. From the early 1990s, when the band first started to perform, till now, their live events have become almost a phenomenon, solidifying DMB's position as among the top touring acts in the globe. Their legacy has been characterized and millions of people have been drawn to their concerts by their dedication to musical improvisation, close relationship with their audience, and relentless quest to challenge live performance limits.

Dave Matthews obviously was not some average rock band when he originally started the band in 1991. Their live performances from the outset were imbued with a spontaneity and vitality unique to many of their peers. DMB used their concerts as a forum for improvisation, allowing their songs to develop and change in real time unlike bands that only replicated their studio recordings note-for--note on stage. This strategy produced an exciting and erratic quality that made every concert seem to be a different event. From their first big tours to their early club gigs, the band rapidly gained a reputation for producing vibrant, surprising performances.

As DMB's appeal developed in the 1990s, so did the size and scope of their live events. Hits like "What Would You Say" and "Crash Into Me," first presented to the world on albums like Under the Table and Dreaming (1994) and Crash (1996), but it was their live shows that really let the band establish a closer connection with their fans. DMB's distinctive sound really blossomed on stage, even although their studio recordings were often rather popular. Their concerts combined rock, jazz, funk, and folk elements, and each one became a dynamic and changing event. Their improvisational style meant that every time a fan saw the band perform, they might anticipate a different rendition of their favorite tunes.

DMB's dedication to stretching the bounds of their live presentations grew increasingly evident as the years passed. With each performance turning into an event in itself, the band started to explore bigger venues and more complex stage configurations. Their live popularity evolved mostly on their capacity to provide the audience an immersive experience. The band's on-stage camaraderie and intensity were indisputable, regardless of the venue—a small club or a stadium With songs like "So Much to Say" and

"Crash Into Me" became mainstays of their live sets, their 1996 album Crash solidified their reputation as one of the best live performers. Still, what kept audiences returning for more was their ability to stretch out these tunes, guiding them via improvisation in fresh directions.

DMB's live presentations started to have a mythological character around this time. The band was forging a shared experience with their audience, not only playing their songs. Every concert turned into a cooperation between the band and the audience, so the room was clearly energetic. The mood was shaped in great part by the audience, which responded to the music and thereby directed the performance. Dave Matthews himself regularly recognized the significance of this engagement, usually complimenting the fans' vitality and excitement. Every performance seemed like a group event where the band and the crowd were co-creating something unique because of their mutual respect and connection.

The live CD Live at Red Rocks 8.15.95, which featured one of the band's most well-known concerts at Colorado's Red Rocks Amphitheatre, proved their capacity to enthrall an audience during live events. The popularity of this album was a major turning point for DMB since it proved the ability of their live performances to surpass the produced content. While those who had not could hear personally what made DMB's live events so unique, those who had attended the concert could revisit the event. Live at Red

Rocks also signaled the start of DMB's policy of distributing live recordings from their events, therefore enabling fans to carry a bit of the concert with them home. This behavior not only increased the demand for their live events but also helped to solidify the belief that DMB's performances defined their band's identity.

DMB had grown to be among the largest live performers worldwide. Major events, their tours drew large numbers of people to venues and amphitheaters all around. The band's popularity grew not just on the caliber of their songs but also on their capacity to provide listeners with a concert experience unique among others. DMB's events celebrated music, community, and spontaneity rather than only presentations. Every performance was a live, breathing entity molded by the particular enthusiasm of the audience and the band's inventiveness.

The band has stayed dedicated to changing their live performances over their history, always looking for fresh and interesting approaches. DMB has constantly sought to improve the live performance experience by including fresh songs into its sets, experimenting with various arrangements, or adding fresh elements of stage design. They have also embraced technology, giving fans the option to stream or buy live recordings of their performances, therefore enabling the enchantment of their concerts to be enjoyed long after the last note has been played.

The foundation of the band's success has been their close relationship with their audience. DMB's live performances, unlike many other artists, seem intimate as though the band is addressing the crowd personally. Their music's improvisational quality as well as the passion of their followers provide an exciting and anticipatory mood. Not only are fans viewers; they are also active participants in the performance, therefore influencing the experience with their vitality and involvement. This kind of active involvement has produced a committed fanbase that has stayed with the band all through the years.

Dave Matthews Band is still a top live act in the world today, attracting sizable audiences and a consistent travel schedule. Their will to offer a distinctive, immersive concert experience guarantees that their live performances will always be an essential component of their legacy. DMB's live events continue to be celebrations of music, community, and the relationship between the band and their fans whether they feature fresh material or revisiting beloved songs.

Dealing with Fame

Dave Matthews has often considered the astounding scale of his explosive ascent to prominence in the 1990s, when the Dave Matthews Band (DMB) moved from performing small venues to packing arenas and stadiums in a shockingly brief period. Often quiet and reflective, Matthews has frankly discussed the difficulties accompanying this degree of success and how he managed the burden of celebrity while preserving his sense of self. His path is a singular story of juggling personal beliefs with the pressures of notoriety, and his style of handling celebrity reveals much about his character and the philosophy that has kept him going over years.

Matthews was thrown into the public in a way he had never anticipated when DMB's 1994 debut album, Under the Table and Dreaming, became a blockbuster success. Hit songs on the album, "What Would You Say" and "Ants Marching," connected with a broad audience right away. The band's addictive live performances and ability to mix several genres helped them to carve out a niche appealing to both mainstream audiences and more specialized, jam-band aficionados, hence fueling their quick rise. Matthews himself has noted in interviews, nevertheless, he was not ready for the public scrutiny and intensive attention that accompanied this rapid popularity.

Matthews has come clean about not having ever aggressively pursued celebrity. Actually, he has frequently said that his nature is more reflective and oriented on intimate ties than on public recognition. Being thrown into the limelight, where his every action would be monitored and criticised, excited and unnerved me simultaneously. Matthews has admitted in interviews the isolating features of popularity, especially the difficulties of preserving true connections while surrounded by individuals who might have hidden reasons or only want to be close to the "star," rather than the actual person. Early on Matthews had to learn to negotiate the conflict between public and private life.

Matthews surrounded himself with a close-knit group of friends and colleagues who helped ground him, thereby managing the demands of celebrity. Among the whirl of their growing celebrity, his bandmates—who he has sometimes characterized as his family—were instrumental in offering support and a sense of normalcy. Matthews has always underlined the value of the band's friendship as their common experience on the road and in the studio produced stability and mutual respect. Matthews's relationship with his fellow artists helped him to keep authenticity in a society too frequently preoccupied with appearances over content.

Matthews has also been candid on how he handled the emotional complexity of celebrity via his songs. Writing songs turned into a means of expression for him to convey the uncertainty, self-doubt, and loneliness sometimes accompanying public life. Many of his songs explore ideas of inner reflection, relationships, and the conflict between public persona and private identification. Even when outside demands grew, his capacity to focus his emotions into his music helped him to stay in control of his life.

Apart from the music itself, Matthews took comfort in his own morals. He has regularly discussed his passion for the natural world and the need to follow his values, which has helped him negotiate the demands of celebrity. Long advocates of social justice and environmental issues, Matthews found meaning in his pursuits that went beyond the surface level of notoriety. Through his participation in several humanitarian projects, like the Bama Works Fund, he has been able to focus his energies toward changing the world, grounding and connecting him to something more than the music business or his public image.

Matthews gained a good feeling of detachment from the public's expectations and the media despite the overwhelming character of celebrity. He has over the years discussed how he learnt to set limits, especially with regard to preserving a personal life. He has been guarding his personal space, making sure his family life stays out of sight. Matthews has frequently stressed the need of having time for himself, away from the continuous pressures of travel and public appearances. Whether they involve spending time with loved ones or withdrawing into nature, far from the curious eyes of the world, he has found comfort in peaceful times.

Matthews's capacity to control celebrity is much enhanced by his self-awareness and readiness to welcome vulnerability. His candor in facing the challenges he has personally and professionally has won him favor from his followers. Matthews has always made it plain that, like everyone else, he sees himself as someone who is learning and developing rather than as superhuman or flawless. Many of his audience value his candor and vulnerability, which have helped him to keep a close relationship with them by means of his own defects confronting attitude.

Matthews's attitude to celebrity also emphasizes his capacity for perspective. He has frequently shown thanks for the achievements he and his band have accomplished as well as for realizing the ephemeral character of celebrity. Matthews has underlined that he stays grounded since he never takes his achievements for granted and that knowledge that celebrity is fleeting helps him. This viewpoint has helped him to keep producing songs in line with his creative vision instead of following trends or striving to keep his star reputation. Matthews has made it very evident that his love of music—rather than the glitz of celebrity—drives him to keep performing and producing.

Matthews has found a careful mix between the pressures of celebrity and his own personal welfare over his career. Matthews has negotiated the demands of popularity in a way that has let him keep his integrity by surrounding himself with a supportive team, following his principles, and using his music as a medium for self-expression. Dave Matthews has stayed a very reflective, grounded, and real person in the world of music, constantly trying to stay true to himself while embracing the possibilities that come with his accomplishment despite the inevitable challenges that accompany celebrity.

Chapter 4

His Journey beyond the Music

Renowned for his musical career with the Dave Matthews Band, Dave Matthews has also explored new artistic vistas and committed major charitable activities outside of the music business. Matthews explored personal and introspective themes on his first solo album, "Some Devil", which won critical praise and a Grammy Award for the eerie song "Gravedigger." His skill set also included acting, where he approached narrative in original ways by filling roles in movies and TV shows. Particularly with his Bama Works Fund, Matthews's charitable endeavors show his great dedication to social and environmental issues, therefore supporting communities and pushing change. Apart from his achievements in his career, Matthews has also negotiated the difficulties of juggling family life with stardom, preserving a grounded and private life apart from his public image. His path outside of the music business exposes a multifarious artist committed to both personal development and world change.

His Solo Journey

With the publication of Some Devil in 2003, a project allowing Dave Matthews to explore his own artistic voice and break away from the restrictions of his work with the Dave Matthews Band (DMB), his solo trip started. Mostly known for his vocals and major songwriter for DMB, Matthews ventured boldly with his first solo album, breaking away from the band's cooperative approach. Some Devil was a very personal record that addressed themes of introspection, sorrow, and self-reflection, portraying a side of Matthews that was sometimes obscured by the louder than life sound of DMB. Apart from positive reviews, the album was a turning point in Matthews' career since it proved his capacity to produce songs on his own terms.

For Matthews, the process of creating Some Devil was intimate and experimental. Although his work with DMB had always been based on teamwork, the solo album let him explore his own feelings and musical ideas more deeply. Though long renowned for his passionate songs, Matthews approached the album's production more actively. He significantly contributed guitar, piano, and even some bass lines to the instrumentation, therefore giving the album a more raw, stripped-down sound. Working closely with producer Stephen Harris—with whom he has a long-standing working relationship—he sought to create a very contemplative and empathetic tone. Some Devil was simple, letting Matthews's voice and words take front stage in the listening experience unlike DMB's more complex configurations.

The sound and tone of the album stood far apart from Matthews' work with DMB. Although the band's songs frequently mixed elements of rock, jazz, and folk with a great sense of improvisation, Some Devil was calmer, darker, and more meditative. The album's themes—heavy in contemplation, coping with loss, personal strife, redemption, and the complexity of human emotions—run through the book. Matthews seems not hesitant to investigate his weaknesses in a manner less obviously clear in his work with DMB. Songs like "Some Devil" and "Save Me" caught the conflict Matthews sometimes felt between his public image and his inner conflicts. His dependably lyrical songs adopted a more intimate and heartfelt tone for this solo work. For many listeners who related to the song "Some Devil," for example, it explores the inner struggle of juggling one's darker side.

Among the defining events of "Some Devil" was the melancholy and eerie song "Gravedigger," which turned out to be a highlight on the record. With a melancholy piano theme and little instrumentation, the song was simple in its approach and matched Matthews' very contemplative lyrics. The song looks at mortality, the passing of time, and the human experience of negotiating death. Though he is excavating graves for others, the gravedigger in the song muses over his own death. Audiences related to Matthews' emotionally charged performance and the introspective character of the song. "Gravedigger" went on to win a Grammy Award for Best Male Rock Vocal Performance in 2004, so attesting to the simplicity of the song's arrangement allowing its great message to resonate more deeply with listeners, proving sometimes less is more when it comes to expressing strong emotions. Though Matthews had previously enjoyed great success with DMB, Some Devil let him break out from the shadow of the band and establish himself as a solo artist. With a raw, sensitive, and hauntingly beautiful performance, Matthews' Grammy victory for "Gravedigger" was evidence of his capacity to emotionally connect with listeners. The appreciation was not only for the song but also for Matthews' development as an artist capable of standing outside of DMB. It was a recognition of his distinct voice and creative capacity apart from his band activities.

Apart from "Gravedigger," the CD included additional noteworthy songs such "So Damn Lucky" and "Crash Into Me." "So Damn Lucky" offered Matthews' songwriting's more positive side. Though some of the other tracks on the album have a darker tone, the song's lively rhythm and hopeful chorus nevertheless really speak to me in terms of contemplation and thankfulness. Matthews investigated the sensation of being "damn lucky"—alive and conscious of the transient character of life. The song's lively quality gave the more sad and reflective tunes that comprised much of Some Devil a counterpoint. Conversely, the modified form of "Crash Into Me" presented an earlier DMB classic in the solo setting, providing a fresh interpretation of the known song with a softer, more personal arrangement. It highlighted Matthews' ability to reimagine his own work and offered listeners another viewpoint on one of the most famous songs of the band.

Matthews' themes on Some Devil expressed his will to face the complexity of personal experience and human nature. Songs on the album explored concepts of self-doubt, love, loss, and redemption. Unafraid to face the discomforts and challenges sometimes overlooked in public life, it was a record that spoke to Matthews' inner workings. Offering listeners a window into his soul, he did not hold back while displaying the darkest sides of his nature. Fans who had come to know Matthews as a reflective, poetic person connected with this rawness. The album's honest lyrics helped him to establish a closer relationship with his listeners by enabling them to identify with his challenges and pleasures.

Some Devil explored Matthews' personal feelings as well as a creative divergence from the sounds and techniques that distinguished his work with DMB. It was a chance for Matthews to venture outside the band's purview and engage in artistic risk in ways he might not have been able to accomplish with a group. It was an opportunity for him to push himself as a solo performer and discover several musical environments. The album confirmed Matthews' capacity to live both inside and outside of the DMB tradition and reflected a strengthening of his artistic abilities. Matthews was able to create his own route while still keeping the deep, poetic qualities that had made him a beloved person in the music business.

Some Devil stayed a turning point in Matthews' career for years to come. It highlighted his capacity to access his feelings and communicate in ways that were both personal and generally relevant. The record demonstrated that Matthews was a multi-dimensional artist capable of producing interesting, thoughtful music on his own terms, not only a singer for DMB. By means of Some Devil, Matthews not only confirmed his position in the music scene but also demonstrated that his creative path was far from finished, with much more to investigate both as a solo performer and within his venerable ensemble.

Acting and Artistic Ventures

Dave Matthews's debut into acting followed naturally from his artistic adaptability and demonstrated his eagerness to try several narrative techniques. Though mostly renowned for his musical career with the Dave Matthews Band (DMB), Matthews's acting parts gave him the chance to flex his creative muscles in fresh and interesting ways. His endeavors in film and television are distinguished by characters that frequently play on his contemplative, occasionally eccentric, nature, therefore enabling him to provide a certain sensitivity to his performances.

Matthews landed his first significant acting job in 2003 on the movie "Where the Red Fern Grows". Matthews portrayed the father of the main character in this family-friendly rendition of Wilson Rawls' classic book—a small child who befriended two dogs. Though Matthews's part was somewhat minor in comparison to the protagonist, the movie was a significant turning point in his acting career since it proved his capacity to give a job warmth and authenticity. This part was well-received and helped Matthews establish himself as an actor with a natural, grounded presence that provided a peek of his potential as a performer apart from music.

Matthews then broadened his acting career with a variety of roles on television and movies. Based on the book by Kate DiCamillo, one of his more well-known movie performances came in 2005 with "Because of Winn-Dixie". Matthews portrayed a weird and withdrawn pet store owner with a soft heart named Otis. The family drama-oriented movie, which revolves on a small child befriending a dog, received compliments on Matthews' performance of Otis for its realism and depth. Matthews added his signature sensitivity to the part, conveying the loneliness of the character but also showing his development as he grew close to the other film stars. His performance served as a reminder of his capacity to arouse compassion and captivate viewers into the universe of his characters.

Matthews's acting technique revolves mostly on his natural, subdued approach to performance. His work sometimes runs counter to the more dramatic, larger-than-life personas prevalent in Hollywood movies. Rather, Matthews prefers jobs that let him be nuanced and introspective, therefore reflecting the softer, more reflective elements that distinguish most of his work. Matthews has talked in interviews about how his acting and music entwine in that both demand sensitivity and honesty. He approaches acting much as he does songwriting—by relating to the core of his character and adding an emotional honesty to the performance.

Matthews portrays the quirky companion of the protagonist in the dark comedy "You Might As Well Live", 2010. Dealing with themes of friendship, grief, and disillusionment, the movie let Matthews bring his eccentricity to a part that would be both funny and poignant. Matthews's inherent ability to give his character warmth combined with the film's dark, pessimistic tone created an engaging performance. It also demonstrated his ability to negotiate more unusual, off-beat characters that strayed from the classic leading-man archetype.

Matthews has appeared in a number of television shows in addition to his movie work. Playing the character "Teddy," a guy suffering with a challenging medical condition, he was a guest star in the television series "House". Once more leveraging his ability to bring empathy and authenticity to the screen, Matthews's modest but poignant performance in the show was Matthews' look on "House" showed his flexibility and ability to balance the more dramatic elements of the show with his own particular taste, even though his part was not a key one.

Although Matthews's acting career has not been as long as his musical one, his attitude to acting is obviously one of great thought and care. Like his music, acting calls for vulnerability and a thorough awareness of the characters he plays. Particularly those requiring sensitivity and subtlety, he gravitates toward parts that let him investigate the emotional complexity of the human experience. Using his own personal events to guide his characters, Matthews constantly strives to bring realism to his performances—in film or on television.

Matthews's acting also fits his method of approaching musical narrative. In interviews, he has explored the similarities between acting and songwriting—both call for a strong emotional dedication to narrative telling and a close relationship to the subject matter. Matthews sees acting as another kind of artistic expression in many respects, enabling him to inhabit people and transmit emotions in ways that accentuate his music. Acting provides Matthews another means to investigate the complexity of human emotions and narrative, not only a means of recognition in another field.

His ability to negotiate acting and music reflects his multifarious creative sensibility. Matthews has never been someone who fits neatly into one box; his move into acting is another instance of his eagerness to push himself and broaden his creative horizons. Sensitive, intellectual, and emotionally rich—qualities of his music—his film and TV roles often mirror these traits, therefore demonstrating that his talents transcend the domain of music. Though his acting career might not be as broad as his work with DMB, Matthews has found a niche for himself in the realm of film and television with understated emotional depth in his performances.

Matthews' method of performing also reveals a readiness to explore other genres and styles and to take chances. From family dramas to dark comedy, Matthews has demonstrated that he is not hesitant to venture beyond his comfort zone and play several kinds of characters. Though less well-known than some of his contemporaries, his films and television work are evidence of his love of narrative and his commitment to investigate uncharted creative directions.

Matthews's acting career ultimately reflects his larger artistic path, one distinguished by a passion for creative expression, emotional honesty, and a readiness to investigate new artistic media. Matthews never fails to enthrall audiences with his capacity to connect on a profoundly personal level whether on stage, in front of a camera, or via the lens of a song. Though not very active, his step into acting adds still another dimension to his varied career and demonstrates that his artistic path is far from constrained within the boundaries of music.

His Act of Philanthropy

Dave Matthews has long been known for his musical ability as well as for his dedication to humanitarian, environmental, and social concerns. Matthews, a well-known public person with much power, has utilized his position to promote many projects consistent with his personal principles, advocate for change, and assist philanthropic activities. The Bama Works Fund, a charitable foundation Matthews founded in 1999 to offer financial support to groups concentrated on a range of causes, including environmental conservation, social justice, and community development, leads first among his humanitarian activities. Matthews has shown a strong will to give back and have a real impact on the world by his philanthropy.

Matthews's main means of philanthropic giving has been the Bama Works Fund. Originally started with the Dave Matthews Band, the foundation supports groups trying to have a good influence on the local environment as well as the larger globe. Originally established to help the Charlottesville, Virginia area—where Matthews has long called home—the fund has expanded to assist projects much beyond the local neighborhood. Emphasizing subjects like education, environmental preservation, and poverty reduction, the Bama Works Fund awards to a broad spectrum of charitable groups. Early on, the foundation funded music education initiatives, helped local infrastructure be built, and gave social services financial aid. With Matthews and his bandmates still collecting money via their tours and other initiatives, the range of its influence grew over time.

Empowering people and communities by means of resources to businesses generating significant, long-lasting transformation is one of the main objectives of the Bama Works Fund. Matthews has been particularly committed to helping grassroots projects aiming at social justice, equality, and opportunity for underprivileged groups. The foundation has given to groups addressing at-risk young people, offering homeless services, and raising mental health consciousness. Matthews has underlined the need of tackling systematic inequality a lot of times, and the humanitarian activities of the Bama Works Fund show his will to build a more fair and equal society.

Matthews has also focused most of his career on the environmental impact; the Bama Works Fund has been crucial in helping initiatives to preserve the earth. Matthews has been a vocal supporter of environmental preservation and sustainable living, and his background has given groups working toward this great support. The Bama Works Fund has sought to increase awareness of the pressing need for environmental action from wildlife preservation to the support of renewable energy.

Matthews's own dedication to sustainability has shown itself in his attempts to lower the Dave Matthews Band's tour carbon footprint by means of recycling, waste reduction, and carbon emissions offsetting programs.

Apart from the Bama Works Fund, Matthews has raised more general awareness of environmental problems using his celebrity profile. To raise knowledge of climate change and the value of sustainable living, he has teamed with several groups, including the environmental campaigning group Earthwatch. Matthews' advocacy covers problems including access to clean water, alternative energy sources, and preservation of natural environments. From on stage to off, his advocacy of environmental problems has been a recurring motif throughout his career. Matthews has shown his commitment to change the world by helping to generate millions of dollars for social and environmental concerns using the Bama Works Fund and other charitable endeavors.

Matthews's participation in activism also spans a range of social concerns, including political activity and support of human rights. He has been very outspoken about issues including racial inequity and immigration reform, and he has utilized his platform to protest policies and practices he feels to be unfair. Matthews has always supported progressive social policies and been steadfast in her support of causes including civil rights and marital equality. He has raised awareness of subjects near and dear to his heart by encouraging others to participate and take action through his writings, interviews, and public appearances.

Matthews and other performers pushed young people to vote and engage in the political process using the tour as a venue. Matthews's commitment to social and political change endured in later years since he regularly discussed issues including economic disparity and climate change. Apart from his songs, he has actively participated in discussions on social reform and policy, therefore using his voice to advocate justice and equality.

Apart from his advocacy, Matthews has assisted groups striving for peace and nonviolence. Being a musician, he has always been drawn to the ability of music to be a tool for good change and has backed groups trying to unite people and advance understanding across political and cultural borders. Matthews has frequently discussed how music can break down boundaries and unite individuals from many walks of life in the name of harmony and peace. Matthews has tried to carry out this idea via his humanitarian work and advocacy, supporting projects that promote peace and collaboration in a society sometimes seeming to be divided.

Matthews has given his time and skills to many charities, so his charitable activities go beyond mere money gifts. He has sponsored many projects aiming at social welfare, health, and education, volunteered at community events, and participated at benefit performances. Matthews has shown his dedication by his humanitarian deeds; he has often remarked that he feels a great need to use his platform for good. From disaster relief to the battle against poverty, his support of causes reflects his conviction in the need of returning to the planet that has helped him all of his career.

Matthews has demonstrated by his charitable activities and advocacy that he is more than just a musician—he is a fervent supporter of environmental and social concerns. In the realm of philanthropic giving and activity, he is well-known for his dedication to the Bama Works Fund, environmental preservation, human rights, and political involvement. Matthews has regularly made a good difference in the world and raised awareness of significant problems using his popularity and clout. His character and conviction in the ability of people to bring about change are demonstrated by his commitment to philanthropy and activity.

Balancing Family and Fame

Dave Matthews has long been well-known for his grounded approach and capacity to keep equilibrium in a life sometimes demanding the limelight. Although Matthews's music career with the Dave Matthews Band (DMB) has garnered him international recognition, he has worked hard to preserve his personal life and given family values top priority among the tumult of popularity. Grounded in the conviction that family comes first, his method of juggling celebrity and responsibility has been based on trying to give his loved ones top priority while negotiating the demands of his public job.

Since 2000, Matthews has been wed to Jennifer Ashley Harper; the two have three children together. Matthews has kept his family life mostly secret throughout his career, preferring to concentrate on his job and personal life free from the public view away from the cameras. His need for privacy has helped him to defend the dignity of his family life from the often intrusive character of celebrity. Matthews talks about his family clearly, showing his dedication to them by regularly stressing the value of family ties and how they give him comfort and foundation in his hectic life.

The Matthews family's way of life is based on the conviction that children ought to grow up in loving and encouraging surroundings free from public eye distractions. Matthews has always underlined the need of being present for his children as they grow up; he has also regarded them as the center of his world.

Matthews has made it a top goal to spend as much time as he can with his family despite the pressures of travel and ongoing media coverage of his career. His wish to provide his children a sense of normalcy even in the face of worldwide celebrity is demonstrated by his keeping his family life out of the spotlight.

Matthews has frequently discussed in interviews how he seeks to strike a balance between his personal life and his job. Although touring and creating music can be taxing, Matthews has found time for his family. He does this, among other things, meticulously schedule the Dave Matthews Band's activities to guarantee enough time for family and rest prior to starting tours. Matthews has discussed the need of finding a good balance between job and personal life and underlined that keeping his own well-being depends on spending time with his kids. He has also underlined how much his wife Jennifer's love and encouragement have helped him negotiate the demands of celebrity and provide emotional stability to enable him to stay focused on what is really important.

Matthews, a parent, has frequently said that his children inspire and bring delight into his life. Though well-known, Matthews is a hands-on dad who enjoys the daily events of parenthood. Matthews values being there in his children's life whether that means going to school events, spending time outside with them, or just savoring quiet times at home. Matthews has also said in the past that he wants to educate his kids moral virtues including kindness, diligence, and honesty so they may pass on significant life lessons. Matthews thinks in leading by example; he emphasizes the need of keeping humility, showing compassion, and constantly scheduling time for the ones most important.

Matthews has admitted the difficulties of keeping that balance as juggling family life with celebrity presents problems. Often it is difficult to keep in touch with loved ones due to frequent travel, long road hours, and public attention. Particularly with regard to the distance from his children and wife, Matthews has detailed the toll traveling can take on a family. Matthews has demonstrated resilience in spite of these obstacles, finding means to keep in touch with his family even while he is far from home. Matthews has made it plain that he wants to stay active in his family's lives no matter how busy his schedule gets—through frequent video chats, messaging, or just scheduling time to be with him off tour.

Matthews's dedication to living in a quite low-key manner, despite his celebrity position, helps one of the ways he has managed the demands of fame while preserving a strong family life. Matthews and his family have settled in the Charlottesville, Virginia area, where they can lead a more subdued, private life than they would in bigger, more celebrity-centric locations like Los Angeles or New York. Matthews has highlighted how crucial it is to him to reside somewhere his family may enjoy solitude and where he may keep ties to the neighborhood. Living in a small town has let Matthews give his kids the kind of childhood he values free from the heavy public scrutiny sometimes associated with living in the limelight.

Matthews's desire to preserve his family's privacy and his dedication to them have also guided his public interaction to be selective.

Choosing to concentrate on his music career and charitable work instead of drawing attention to his personal life, he has regularly kept his family life out of the headlines. Matthews has been careful to protect his loved ones from needless exposure and has repeatedly voiced annoyance with the intracity of celebrity culture. This strategy has helped Matthews stay in balance, separating his public from personal life and shielding his family from the sometimes brutal nature of celebrity scrutiny.

Matthews has been fervently committed to both family and celebrity despite the difficulties in juggling them. His family is central to his life; he has developed his work around the conviction that success is about preserving healthy connections and a feeling of purpose rather than only about fame or wealth. Matthews's speech about his loved ones clearly shows his commitment to his family; also, his capacity to give them first priority in spite of professional demands reveals his moral and character strength. Matthews has found a way to negotiate the world of celebrity while being true to his family values by separating his business from personal life and maintaining anchored in his connections.

Chapter 5

The Legacy of Dave Matthews

The music business has been permanently changed by Dave Matthews and his band, the Dave Matthews Band (DMB), which influences modern rock and inspires numerous musicians working in several genres. Well-known for their original mix of rock, jazz, folk, and blues, DMB has a powerful live presence and improvisational style. Thanks in significant part to his distinctive voice and imaginative guitar techniques, Matthews is a major participant in modern music; his thoughtful lyrics appeal to listeners on a deep emotional level.

DMB's global popularity has shaped international music trends and introduced its broad blend to listeners all around by virtue of its ability to traverse boundaries and cultures. Although they first emerged in the early 1990s, the band's appeal is timeless since they constantly enthrall next generations of fans while maintaining a dedicated following from their early years.Matthews has exhibited pride in his path and value in the growth of his band and personally while thinking about his profession. Looking forward, his dedication to his vocation and continuous contributions to the music scene ensure that his legacy will inspire for many years to come.

His Impact on the Music Industry

Through his unique sound, creative performances, and ongoing influence on contemporary rock, Dave Matthews has fundamentally changed the music business. As Dave Matthews Band (DMB) frontman, he developed a musical style that seemed exciting and approachable by blending rock, jazz, folk, and world music in a way that seemed tough to explain. Their unique instrumentation—which included violin and saxophone—created a multi-layered sound especially in the 1990s. Well-known pieces of that era were songs like "Under the Table and Dreaming" and "Crash", which highlights Matthews' ability to mix sophisticated arrangements with profoundly emotional lyrics.

Matthews's songs reinforced his reputation. Audiences will find great resonance with his songs, which probe common concerns including love, death, social justice, and human development. Songs like "Crash into Me," "Ants Marching," and "Gravedigger" remain classic for their provocative stories as much as for their melodies. Many musicians have been motivated to approach their own work with the same depth and honesty by his capacity to create songs that mix introspection with universal appeal.

Matthews's attitude to live music is among his most important offerings to the field. Celebrated for its improvisational approach, the Dave Matthews Band presents different takes of their songs every concert. This focus on spontaneity and musicianship changed the live music experience and helped to build a loyal audience that appreciates the special vitality of every concert. Matthews showed that touring might be a strong basis for a long music career by giving live involvement top priority over conventional radio performance. His success in this field inspired other musicians to concentrate on live performance as a main component of their own creative paths, therefore changing the dynamics in the business to favor real audience interactions.

The Dave Matthews Band became among the best-selling artists of all time despite their unusual sound since they had amazing commercial success. Top charts and critical praise for albums including "Before These Crowded Streets" and "Everyday" demonstrated that creative music could flourish in a crowded market. Matthews's ability to become well-known without compromising artistic integrity motivated other musicians to stick to their creative goals even under commercial demands.

Matthews and his band also embraced a forward-looking independent attitude ahead of their day. They model handling the complexity of the music business by self-producing live recordings and keeping creative ownership over their music. Their innovative approaches to ticket sales, online fan interaction, and music distribution affected how performers interact with fans and maintain their careers in a fast changing sector.

Dave Matthews's impact goes beyond his own career to the several musicians that name him as inspiration. From Matthews' introspective songwriting, creative guitar methods, and dramatic stage presence, musicians like John Mayer, Ed Sheeran, and Jason Mraz have borrowed from Other artists have been inspired to challenge limits and take artistic chances by his eagerness to play with difficult time signatures, unusual chord progressions, and genre-blending arrangements.

Apart from motivating individual musicians, Matthews has changed more general musical trends. Their capacity to cross genres and appeal to a wide range of listeners proved that music outside of conventional labels could get both critical and financial recognition.

Matthews's influence transcends only music. He is a well-known voice in artist activity because of his commitment to social and environmental issues. Working with groups like Farm Aid, Live Earth, and the Nature Conservancy, he has utilized his position to highlight sustainability, poverty, and climate change. Other musicians have been motivated by this dedication to use their influence for social benefit, hence promoting an activist culture inside the music business.

Dave Matthews's many contributions to the music business demonstrate his sincerity, inventiveness, and artistic sensibility. While his ability to negotiate the business on his terms has been a model for innumerable musicians, his unique musical style and transforming attitude to live performance have left an enduring impression on current rock. Matthews has left a legacy that inspires artists and supporters even now by following his artistic vision and questioning accepted wisdom. His impact will always be a lighthouse helping to shape music for next generations.

His Life as a Global Phenomenon

Dave Matthews's existence as a worldwide sensation is closely entwined with the Dave Matthews Band's (DMB) international popularity and their significant impact on world music trends. From its 1991 founding, the band broke across geographical and cultural barriers to create a loyal following that went much beyond the US. They were a singular force in modern music since their unique mix of rock, jazz, folk, and world music connected listeners all around.

The band appeals to people because they can produce original yet generally relevant songs. Born in South Africa and reared in the United States and the United Kingdom, Matthews brought to his work a varied cultural viewpoint. The band's sound was shaped by their worldwide background, which included components of several musical traditions into their works. Not only for their lyrical profundity but also for their capacity to relate to listeners from many backgrounds, songs like "Crash into Me" and "Ants Marching" became anthems.

International trips by DMB were absolutely vital in confirming their worldwide phenomenon status. Renowned for their explosive live shows, the band often produced vibrant and original events attracting large audiences in Europe, Asia, and beyond. Every performance was an event, highlighting their improvisational skills and generating a feeling of uniqueness that won viewers all around over likeness. Their dedication to live music shows how performance could be a transforming and universal language, therefore redefining travel.

The band's genre-blending approach clearly influences world music trends since it encouraged musicians all around to try out several approaches. DMB broke genre boundaries by including elements of African rhythms, jazz improvisation, and acoustic-driven rock, therefore motivating musicians to embrace cultural and stylistic variety in their work. A generation of global artists driven by this openness to innovation has helped world music to become a major player in the business.

Matthews's personal narrative added even more attraction from all around. Rising to popularity in the United States, he became a symbol of cross-cultural success as a native South African who embodied the possibilities of combining traditions to produce something special. His charitable activities, especially in relation to social and environmental concerns, also connected globally and matched his artistic ability to a more general goal appealing to supporters all around.

The band's deliberate application of newly developed technologies helped to support their worldwide success. Early use of digital distribution and online fan involvement let them more successfully reach worldwide audiences, therefore establishing a standard for how musicians might use technology to increase their audience. Distributed globally, their live albums and concert recordings become mainstay for those appreciating the spontaneity and sincerity of their performances.

The worldwide phenomenon status of the Dave Matthews Band is evidence of their capacity to produce songs that crosses boundaries and ties individuals. Their combination of several inspirations and adherence to their artistic vision helped define world music trends and motivated a fresh generation of musicians to challenge accepted limits. Matthews's leadership and cultural viewpoint enhanced this influence so that the legacy of the band would remain firmly ingrained in the fabric of contemporary worldwide music.

His Band's Timeless Attractive Power

The Dave Matthews Band's (DMB) ageless appeal is evidence of their capacity to relate to listeners of many generations. The band has been relevant in a fast shifting music scene for more than thirty years, regularly attracting fresh listeners while keeping a committed core fanbase. Their original sound, creative live presentations, and universal themes in their music help to explain their ongoing appeal.

DMB has always been unique for combining rock, jazz, folk, and world music. From the release of their breakthrough album, Under the Table and Dreaming, in 1994, to their most recent efforts, the band's survival has been mostly dependent on their capacity to modify their sound while nevertheless honoring their beginnings. Appealing to both long-time fans and newer listeners discovering their music for the first time, tracks including "Ants Marching," "Crash into Me," and "Grey Street" remain as relevant today as they were at their release.

Often examining themes of love, life, loss, and hope, their songs have a timeless quality that speaks to people at all phases of life. Whether a fan finds solace in the reflective tone of "The Space Between," or interprets "Two Step" as a call to live completely, DMB's music changes in meaning as listeners develop. This emotional depth guarantees that their songs will always be current, touching both fresh listeners and those who first heard them decades ago.

Another secret to the band's enduring appeal has been their dedication to live shows. Celebrated for their improvisational approach, no two DMB events are ever exactly the same. Attracted by the thrill of hearing known songs in novel, surprising arrangements, fans typically visit several shows. Their music is energetic and interesting because of its spontaneity, which fosters camaraderie among listeners who have shared the experience of these special events. Parents who grew up listening to DMB have brought their kids to the band throughout the years, building a multigenerational following bound by a passion for the live music experience.

DMB's capacity to negotiate shifting industry conditions has also helped to explain its ongoing importance. The band changed with the music business to embrace digital distribution, streaming platforms, and social media so that younger listeners could find their music. To appeal to both elderly fans who treasure these records and new listeners ready to see their legendary performances, they also kept their custom of producing live albums and concert recordings.

The band's ageless appeal has been enhanced even more by their readiness to develop artistically without offending their following. While more recent efforts have returned and reinterpreted their hallmark sound, albums like Before These Crowded Streets stretched creative limits. This harmony of familiarity and experimentation guarantees that their music stays fresh while respecting the aspects that first appeal to their listeners.

The comprehensive audience of DMB also reflects their timelessness. With its varied influences and general appeal, their music draws listeners from many backgrounds and age groups. At their concerts, it is not unusual to find attendees spanning decades bonded by a love of the band's artistry. DMB's reputation as one of the most beloved acts in modern music has been preserved in part by this capacity to engage such a large audience.

The Dave Matthews Band's capacity to remain relevant over decades ultimately boils down to their genuineness and dedication to their art. The band has created a legacy that goes beyond trends by writing songs that appeal to universal human experiences and delivering them with unmatched intensity and emotion. For millions of people, their songs have evolved into a soundtrack for life, entwining with their memories and experiences both old and new. This ongoing link guarantees that DMB's songs will inspire and unite next generations for years to come.

Inspiring the young Musicians

For many new musicians, Dave Matthews has become a model of innovation, sincerity, and tenacity in the music business. His path, distinguished by a unique voice and a relentless dedication to artistry, speaks to young musicians trying to find their way in an often difficult sector.

Matthews's technique to songwriting is among the most important things he has influenced young musicians on. Renowned for his reflective and poetic songs, he has demonstrated that music can be both very personal and generally applicable. Songs like "Crash into Me" and "The Space Between" show how a strong narrative may transform a song from simple enjoyment into a communal emotional experience. Young musicians have been motivated to approach their songwriting with more depth and authenticity by Matthews's ability to spin ideas of love, struggle, and hope into his work.

For upcoming musicians, his creative guitar approaches have also been a revelation. Matthews's use of unusual chords, sophisticated rhythms, and deft finger-picking techniques questions established guitar playing techniques. Rooted on experimentation, his approach has inspired young musicians to challenge limits and investigate novel opportunities with their instruments. Matthews has motivated a generation of guitarists to concentrate on both accuracy and inventiveness in their trade by proving that technical ability can coexist with emotional resonance.

Matthews's focus on teamwork has affected younger artists especially. Celebrated for their dynamic interaction among members, the Dave Matthews Band uses each instrument to provide a different voice to the whole sound. Aspiring artists have been inspired by this cooperative attitude to value group efforts and the contributions of others in producing something more than the sum of its components. Matthews's regard for his bandmates' abilities reminds us of the need for humility and teamwork in creative projects.

Apart from his artistic success, Matthews's genuineness and fortitude against industry demands have motivated upcoming musicians to stay loyal to their own selves. He has shown that authenticity can have a long-lasting effect by regularly giving artistic freedom top priority over financial success. Rising artists have been empowered by this unwavering dedication to his vision to challenge convention, follow their own artistic voices, and trust their intuition.

Matthews's career emphasizes especially the value of live performance as a means of connection and development. His famed concerts, marked by spontaneity and improvisation, show how live music may establish close relationships between musicians and listeners. This reminds young musicians of the transforming power of performance and the need of interacting really with audiences.

Moreover, Matthews's path from modest origins to worldwide recognition emphasizes the need for endurance. His success came from constant hard effort, dedication, and a strong love of his trade rather than from magic overnight. Young artists confronting their challenges will find great inspiration in this story of tenacity since it reminds them that success is usually the result of tenacity and constant dedication.

Beyond music, Matthews' impact motivates young musicians to use their venues to effect constructive change. His commitment to environmental and social issues has demonstrated how potent performers of advocacy can be. Matthews encourages future artists to match their work with their ideals by showing how to blend personal expression with a feeling of responsibility to the surroundings.

Dave Matthews's influence on new musicians stems ultimately from his capacity for setting an example. By way of his talent, inventiveness, and integrity, he has demonstrated that music is not only a vocation but also a means of connecting with people, self-expression, and long-lasting impact. Young musicians look to him not only for inspiration but also as a reminder that honesty and passion one brings to their field define success rather than fame or riches.

The Conclusion

Celebrated musician, songwriter, and actor Dave's life and work have permanently changed the music scene. Born in Johannesburg, South Africa, he grew up surrounded in a culturally varied setting that would later shape his own creative voice. His family travelled often, living in the United States and the United Kingdom among other countries. These early encounters exposed him to a range of musical genres and traditions, hence forming his varied taste and ultimate ambition to work in music.

Eventually Matthews' family moved to Charlottesville, Virginia, where his love of music blossomed. Working several odd jobs, including bartender, he started to network with local artists and hone his guitar and songwriting techniques. The active music culture of Charlottesville turned into a major launching pad for his career. He started the Dave Matthews Band there, assembling a group of gifted musicians each adding something special to the sound of the band.

Matthews imagined from the start a band that broke through traditional categories. The Dave Matthews Band developed a reputation for their unique fusion of world music, jazz, folk, and rock inspirations. Their live presentations are distinguished from others in modern acts by their improvisation and high-energy dynamics. Their debut album, Under the Table and Dreaming, shot them to prominence and won them a devoted following as well as general praise. The album's popularity spoke to the band's capacity to produce inventive yet approachable music.

Matthews and his band started to appeal to listeners all around as they grew well-known. Celebrated for their reflective lyrics and complex musical arrangements, tracks like "Crash into Me," "Ants Marching," and "Satellite" became mainstays of the contemporary rock era. Listeners of all ages could relate to the band's ability to create songs with ideas of love, grief, and personal development. Matthews became a top voice in modern music thanks in large part to this global appeal.

Matthews worked on other artistic projects even when his career with the band was flourishing. Showcasing his artistic flexibility, he starred in movies and on television. Music remained his main love and release even if he was a successful actor. His dedication to authenticity and his reluctance to compromise his creative vision became characteristics of his work, therefore garnering him respect not just from peers in the business but also from fans.

Matthews's charitable attitude is among his strongest suits. Over his career, he has participated actively in many humanitarian endeavors, mostly those aimed at social justice and environmental sustainability. Using their position, Matthews and his band have brought attention to important concerns, organized benefit events, and backed projects meant to bring about good change. His commitment to these issues has strengthened his reputation as an artist who motivates action in addition to entertainment value.

Reputed for providing explosive live performances, the Dave Matthews Band became a worldwide sensation. Attached by a common respect of the band's skill and vitality, their concerts drew listeners from all walks of life. Their ongoing appeal was much influenced by Matthews' focus on live music as a transforming event. The band regularly packed theaters and outdoor spaces over years, building a feeling of camaraderie among their audience that cut across generational lines.

The impact of Matthews on the music business goes much beyond his own output. Songwriter and performer he has motivated many other artists to embrace originality in their work, try other genres, and embrace creativity. Aspiring and seasoned musicians have been permanently changed by his creative guitar methods, lyrical language, and dedication to group projects. Success in music, he has demonstrated, is about creating deep connections via art as much as about financial success.Globally recognized as a symbol, Matthews has stayed relevant over decades. His ability to remain true to his roots and adjust to shifting industry trends guarantees that listeners of both old and new will find resonance in his music. His career is evidence of the strength of passion, tenacity, and keeping authenticity in the face of adversity.

Matthews's enormous contributions to music and his capacity to really connect with people define his legacy today. His remarkable career with the Dave Matthews Band, his philanthropy, and his influence on younger musicians have confirmed his status as a beloved person in modern music. From her hometown of Charlottesville, this young singer's explosive ascent to prominence is an inspiration about the transforming power of music and the need of never letting up.

as podcast episodes, to various platforms and directories. Your podcast's RSS feed is the link or URL that contains all the necessary information about your podcast, including episode titles, descriptions, and audio files. Hosting platforms generate and manage your podcast's RSS feed, allowing you to distribute your episodes to various podcast directories.

5. ID3 Tags: ID3 tags are metadata tags embedded within your podcast audio file that provide information about the episode, such as the title, artist, album, genre, and artwork. These tags help organize and categorize your podcast episodes, making it easier for podcast players and directories to display and search for your content. It's important to fill out the ID3 tags accurately to ensure proper recognition and presentation of your podcast.

6. Subscribers vs. Downloads: Subscribers refer to individuals who have subscribed to your podcast and regularly receive new episodes. Downloads, on the other hand, represent the number of times your podcast episodes have been downloaded or streamed. While subscribers indicate a loyal and engaged audience, downloads reflect the overall reach and popularity of your podcast.

7. Call-to-Action (CTA): A call-to-action is a statement or directive that prompts your listeners to take a specific action after listening to your podcast episode. This can include subscribing to your podcast, leaving a

review, visiting your website, joining your mailing list, or purchasing a product or service. CTAs are crucial for audience engagement, building a community, and converting listeners into loyal fans or customers.

8. Monetization: Monetization refers to the process of generating revenue from your podcast. There are several ways to monetize your podcast, including sponsorships, advertisements, merchandise sales, crowdfunding, affiliate marketing, and paid memberships or subscriptions. It's important to explore different monetization strategies that align with your podcast's niche and target audience.

9. Podfade: Podfade refers to the phenomenon where a podcast gradually loses momentum and eventually stops producing new episodes. It can occur due to various reasons, such as lack of time, motivation, or audience growth. To avoid podfade, it's essential to stay consistent, engage with your audience, continuously improve your content, and explore strategies to sustain your podcast in the long run.

10. RSS Redirect: An RSS redirect is a tool or feature provided by some hosting platforms that allows you to redirect your podcast's RSS feed from one hosting platform to another. This is useful if you decide to switch hosting providers without losing your subscribers or having to manually update your podcast's RSS feed in various directories.

Decoding Technical Jargon: Understanding Bitrate and Show Notes

If you're new to the world of podcasting, you've probably come across terms like bitrate and show notes. But what do they actually mean? In this section, we'll decode some of the technical jargon that often comes up in podcasting discussions.

Let's start with bitrate. Bitrate refers to the amount of data processed or transmitted per unit of time in your podcast audio. It essentially determines the audio quality and file size of your episodes. A higher bitrate generally means better audio quality, but it also results in larger file sizes. On the other hand, a lower bitrate may compromise the audio quality but can lead to smaller file sizes.

When it comes to choosing a bitrate for your podcast, it's important to strike a balance between audio quality and file size. Common bitrates for podcasts range from 64kbps to 192kbps, depending on your preference and any limitations set by your hosting platform. Keep in mind that higher bitrates can be more demanding in terms of storage space and internet bandwidth, so consider your audience's needs and your own resources when making a decision.

Next up, let's demystify show notes. Show notes are written summaries or outlines of your podcast episodes. They provide listeners with additional information, links, and references related to the episode's content. Show notes are an essential part of engaging your audience, improving search engine optimization (SEO), and making it easier for listeners to find and reference specific topics discussed in the episode.

When creating show notes, it's important to include key talking points, resources mentioned in the episode, and any relevant links. Show notes can range from a simple bulleted list to a detailed transcript, depending on your preference and the nature of your podcast. Including timestamps in your show notes can also be helpful for listeners who want to jump to specific sections of your episode.

Apart from helping your audience, show notes can also benefit you as a podcaster. They serve as a handy reference for future episodes, allowing you to build on previous discussions or provide updates on previously mentioned topics. Additionally, show notes can be repurposed as blog posts or social media content, giving your podcast more exposure and allowing you to reach a wider audience.

Understanding these technical terms, such as bitrate and show notes, will help you navigate the world of podcasting with confidence. By making informed decisions about your bitrate, you can ensure that your audio quality matches your desired standards while taking into account storage and bandwidth limitations. And by crafting detailed show notes, you can enhance the listener experience and provide valuable information beyond the audio itself.

Remember, podcasting is not just about the technical aspects. It's also about connecting with your audience, sharing valuable content, and building a community. So, embrace these technical terms, but don't forget the importance of creating engaging and informative episodes that resonate with your listeners.